Teen Mothers

Raising a Baby

By Julie K. Endersbe, MEd

Consultant:
Patricia Flanagan, MD
Assistant Professor, Pediatrics
Brown University, Providence, Rhode Island

Board of Directors, National Organization of
Adolescent Pregnancy, Parenting, and Prevention

Perspectives on Healthy Sexuality

LifeMatters
an imprint of Capstone Press
Mankato, Minnesota

LifeMatters books are published by Capstone Press
818 North Willow Street • Mankato, Minnesota 56001
http://www.capstone-press.com

Printed in the United States of America

Library of Congress Cataloging-in-Publication Data

Endersbe, Julie.
   Teen mothers: raising a baby / Julie Endersbe.
     p. cm. — (Perspectives on healthy sexuality)
   Includes bibliographical references and index.
   Summary: Discusses problems and dilemmas faced by teenage females when they become mothers and identifies options and solutions available to them.
   ISBN 0-7368-0270-3 (book). — ISBN 0-7368-0293-2 (series)
   1. Teenage mothers Juvenile literature. 2. Teenage pregnancy Juvenile literature. 3. Infants—Care Juvenile literature.
   [1. Teenage mothers. 2. Pregnancy. 3. Babies.] I. Title.
   II. Series: Endersbe, Julie. Perspectives on healthy sexuality.
   HQ759.4.E53 2000
   306.874´3—dc21   99-29761
                    CIP

Staff Credits

Anne Heller, editor; Adam Lazar, designer; Heidi Schoof, photo researcher

Photo Credits

Cover: ©PhotoDisc/Barbara Penoyar
FPG International/©Ron Chapple, 7; ©Telegraph Colour Library, 12; ©Michael Hart, 19; ©Bruce Byers, 23; ©Bill Losh, 9
International Stock/©Vincent Graziani, 44; ©James Davis, 58; ©Mimi Cotter, 38
Photo Network/©Karen Holsinger Mullen, 14; ©Eric R. Berndt, 21, 34; ©Dennis MacDonald, 56
Unicorn Stock Photos/©Eric R. Berndt, 27, 37; ©Jeff Greenberg, 42; ©Tommy Dodson, 48; ©Rich Baker, 51
Uniphoto Picture Agency/©Patrick L. Pfister, 28
Visuals Unlimited/©Erwin C. "Bud" Nielsen, 29

A 0 9 8 7 6 5 4 3 2 1

Table of Contents

Chapter Overview

Almost 500,000 babies are born to teen mothers each year.

Females begin menstruating around age 12 but may not marry until around age 25. A female teen's body is ready to reproduce, but she may not be ready to parent.

It is important to make sure about a pregnancy at a local clinic or doctor's office. When the pregnancy is confirmed, options can be discussed. If you decide to carry the baby to term, prenatal visits should be scheduled to ensure a healthy pregnancy.

The baby's father is important. He needs to be involved during pregnancy, birth, and parenting even if the parents are no longer dating.

It takes commitment to keep and raise a baby. Parenting requires a lot of work and sacrifices.

Chapter 1

Finding Out You're Pregnant

I was really surprised when I found out I **Jametta, Age 16** was pregnant. I had my period. It only lasted two days and was very light, but my breasts were so sore. I couldn't stand certain smells. It was like I could smell every odor in a room. It made me sick. I threw up once in my friend's car. I couldn't stand the smell of her cigarette smoke.

My sister was the first one who noticed the signs that I could be pregnant. She took me to buy a home pregnancy test. I was shocked when it turned out positive. I thought it was impossible to get pregnant the first time you had sex. I couldn't believe it.

The number of babies born to teens is slowly going down. Even so, nearly 900,000 teens become pregnant each year in the United States. Teens actually give birth to almost 500,000 babies each year. The number of teens who use condoms to prevent pregnancy is rising. In fact, 78 percent of all teens use a contraceptive the first time they have sexual intercourse. A contraceptive is a method to prevent pregnancy. Many teens also use condoms to prevent sexually transmitted diseases like AIDS.

Why Are Teens Getting Pregnant?

Teens have gotten pregnant for hundreds of years. Today, more teens have sexual intercourse than in years past. At the same time, the age at which women marry has changed. In the 1950s, women commonly married at age 18 or 19. Today, the average age at which women marry is 25. Girls get their first period, however, around age 12.

There is a long gap between a girl's first period and marriage. A young woman's body is able to produce children at age 12. Hormones, the chemicals that control her body functions, send out strong messages. As a result, a young girl has normal thoughts and feelings about sexuality. It is not normal, however, for a 12-year-old to become a mother. She is still learning to take care of herself. This makes the issue complex.

The most common age for teen pregnancy is 18 or 19. At age 19, almost three-fourths of teen women have had sexual intercourse. Young women have several options when they become pregnant. Depending on how far along the pregnancy is, one option may be to end the pregnancy. Some young women decide to give birth to the baby and then have it adopted. Another option is to keep and raise the baby. This book is about the last option.

Carmen, Age 18

I was pregnant at age 15. My boyfriend didn't want to keep the baby. I did not believe in abortion. My aunt suggested adoption. But I was already five months pregnant. I could feel the baby move inside me. I made a decision to raise this baby.

I needed my boyfriend's help. I knew how hard it would be to do it alone. We started making a plan. We talked about school and work. He is going to night school and working full time. I am getting my high school diploma. It's been hard—really hard. But we are going to make it work for our child.

Making Sure of the Pregnancy

New methods make it easy to be sure about a pregnancy. People can purchase a home pregnancy test at most drugstores. A home pregnancy test is fast and affordable. The test is done on a woman's urine. A positive result means she is pregnant.

Some early signs of pregnancy are:

- swollen or tender breasts
- a missed or late period
- light spotting before or after a period
- an extremely tired feeling
- the need to urinate more often
- feelings of nausea
- a heightened sense of smell

Next a pregnancy should be confirmed at a clinic or hospital. Health care workers ask a woman to give a sample of urine. It takes just minutes to test and confirm the pregnancy. A trip to the clinic provides a time to discuss options with the health care provider. It also allows time to set up doctor visits. Prenatal visits happen at regular times before the birth. At the visits, the health of the mother and her unborn baby is checked.

The Baby's Father

A young woman does not get pregnant alone. It also takes a man and his sperm, or sex cells, to create a baby. A pregnancy changes the relationship between the mother and the baby's father. Yet it is important to communicate with the father. He has a right to know he has fathered a child. Children have the right to get to know their father.

It is important to be honest with the father. He needs to understand what is happening. He may not be prepared to be a father. Even so, he needs to take responsibility for his baby. He needs time to prepare for the birth as much as the mother does.

It can be an emotional moment when a young woman learns she is pregnant. Teen moms who are honest with the dad have an easier time. It is also easier if they surround themselves with good support from others. They need to tell one or more supportive adults in their life about the pregnancy.

Making the Commitment to the Baby

Decisions can be hard to make when a pregnancy is unplanned. A young woman who becomes pregnant must choose whether to parent. Choosing to parent requires a lot of work. She must be ready to make sacrifices. The birth of a baby puts great demands on a parent's time, energy, and money. The new baby must come first. A baby affects all parts of a teen mother's life.

Points to Consider

There is a long gap between the age when most girls get their first period and when they marry. Do you think this causes problems? Why or why not?

Do you know teens who have become parents? How did they arrive at the decision to parent?

Why is it important to make sure of a pregnancy at a clinic or hospital?

What role can a father play in a pregnancy?

Chapter Overview

Teen moms must be honest about an unplanned pregnancy. Sharing the news with their own parents is important.

Teen mothers need strong support systems. Often adult parents are a pregnant teen's best support.

A teen pregnancy affects friendships and relationships in school and the community. A teen mom may no longer feel comfortable with these groups.

A teen mom may become frustrated with the father of her baby. Even so, she still may need to include him in the baby's life.

Chapter 2

Dealing With Family and Community

Teens often feel scared to tell their parents about an unplanned pregnancy. Most teens do, however, share the news of pregnancy with their parents. The news can be disappointing for parents to hear. Parents may feel as if they have failed. They know the future will be difficult for their teen. They realize some goals will take longer for their teen to attain.

I thought my mom was going to scream **Patty, Age 17** when I told her I was pregnant. She turned all red and looked like a cartoon character ready to explode. I think she was counting to one million in her head.

Two weeks later she was fine. She was still upset, but she never yelled at me. She never made me feel like a failure. She went with me to all my prenatal visits. She quit buying pop. She made sure I had a good meal at dinnertime. At night, she rubbed my feet while we watched videos of me growing up. She has stuck with me through this.

Healthy Support Systems

Teen mothers need a good support system. Many young moms find this support in their parents. Parents, however, may need time to accept a teen pregnancy. When parents are ready, they can be of great help. They can provide shelter for the mother. They can help with doctor's appointments and birthing classes. Parents also can be good listeners.

Friendships can change during a pregnancy. Many young mothers feel alone. Friends may stop calling. A transition or change begins. A teen finds out who the important friends are in her life. Sometimes they may not be the most likely people.

"Having a baby had a huge impact on my life. Everything I do now is so much harder. I wanted to go to college. I can't even go out after school and hang with my friends. I would definitely tell other teens to wait until they've finished school and done the things they really want to do."
—Sandee, age 17

This change helps teens learn how to decide what is important. It may no longer be clothes or party choices. Parenting is much more important than these choices. Pregnant teens must learn how to make sacrifices. They must learn how to put the child first. This is hard for a teenager. Some still feel like a child themselves.

The School Climate

School may become an unpleasant place. Sometimes students may insult or harass a pregnant or parenting teen. They may invade a pregnant teen's space by touching her stomach. A teen mom has to make choices about what she can or can't do. She may feel left out or different as a result.

Some teen moms decide to attend a different school. Some cities have a smaller school for pregnant or parenting teens. These schools are called alternative learning centers. They provide a flexible and often more accepting place for teens to finish school. Some of these schools include a day care center. The young mother, and sometimes the father, can see the baby during the day. This contact is good for the parents and the baby.

It is important to try to keep attending school as long as possible. This is still important even if the community doesn't have an alternative learning center. Staying in school is much easier to do before the baby is born than it is afterward.

Finding a Place in the Community

The community in which people live should be a safe place for a child to grow up. Not everyone, however, is part of a caring community. Like school, the community may feel unpleasant. People may insult pregnant teens. They may have a negative opinion of those young women.

I was shopping for baby clothes. Two older **Mao, Age 18** women were near me. I could hear them. They were not talking softly. They said I was disgusting. They said I would live off welfare for the rest of my life. They said I was a failure and they felt sorry for my baby.

These women don't know me. I am working hard for my baby. I am starting college next semester. I want a good life for my baby. I looked at them and held my head up. I left that store and didn't look back.

"It's Not Fair!"

Many teen moms feel anger toward the father of the baby. It appears the father has few changes in his life. The pregnancy does not physically change him. He may not be left out or alone. This can be frustrating for a teen mom.

Teen moms may have feelings of failure. Many young women find themselves alone. They believe their boyfriend will help them during the pregnancy. The father of the baby, however, may walk out. He may not be ready to parent.

Young women get pregnant for different reasons. Here are some reasons young teens give.

Teen
Talk

"I needed a way to get out of my house."

"I didn't think it would happen to me."

"He said if I loved him, I should show him by having sex."

"I thought it would bring my boyfriend and me closer together."

"I wanted a baby so I could have someone to love me."

It is easier for the male to leave a pregnancy. He does not carry the baby. This situation has a great effect on the mother. She may feel sad. She may choose to stop eating. She may choose to drink or smoke. These are unhealthy choices for her and her baby.

Feeling Hopeful

It is important to find hope. Young mothers need to have a good support system. They need to surround themselves with good people. A father's involvement is important to the mother and child. Sometimes he chooses not to be around. Even so, it is important for a teen mom to communicate with the father. Raising a child alone is hard work.

Points to Consider

Why is it important for a teen to share the news of a pregnancy with her parents?

Describe ways a teen mom could form a support system.

How do you think school would be different for you if an unplanned pregnancy occurred?

What role should a father play in a pregnancy?

Chapter Overview

Babies need a healthy mother for normal prenatal development.

Good care before the birth of a baby is important. Regular prenatal doctor visits, a good diet, exercise, and rest all produce a healthy baby.

The behavior of both the mother and the father can hurt the fetus.

Common dangers such as x-rays, medicines, and lead can be harmful to the fetus.

Chapter 3

Prenatal Care

Prenatal care occurs before the birth of a baby. A mother can do several things during this time to prepare for motherhood. She can learn how to be a good parent. Regular exercise and plenty of rest help to prepare her body for childbirth.

Healthy foods also prepare a pregnant woman's body. Good food nourishes the developing fetus, or unborn baby. Healthy nutrition especially includes getting enough iron and calcium daily. Eating properly ensures a good weight gain during pregnancy. The mother must stop using tobacco, alcohol, and other drugs. A mother also should visit her doctor regularly. A fetus needs a healthy mother for normal development.

Normal weight gain during pregnancy is between 25 and 35 pounds. Young women who gain fewer than 20 pounds may put their baby at risk. Babies who weigh too little at birth may have delayed growth and immature development.

Some pregnant teens see their family doctor. Others see an obstetrician, or a doctor who treats pregnant women. The doctor may be on call for the birth of the baby. Other teens may choose to see a nurse-midwife. A midwife is not a licensed doctor but is an expert at labor and delivery. A midwife can monitor all prenatal visits just like a doctor does. He or she also can deliver the baby.

Emily, Age 19

My sister had a baby a few years ago. She wanted to see a midwife. Our family doctor said that was fine. She had a pretty normal pregnancy. I was there for the birth of her baby. The midwife spent so much time in the room. She really helped my sister and her husband.

When I got pregnant, the doctor said I was "high risk." The doctor thought it would be best to keep seeing her. I've had to go in for a lot of extra appointments. My blood pressure gets really high. Sometimes I have to stay home from school and just lay around. But my doctor thinks the birth will go okay.

Prenatal Visits

Prenatal visits are important to the health of a baby. The doctor checks the mother's weight and blood pressure and measures her belly. The doctor also monitors the baby's heartbeat. These visits help ensure a healthy pregnancy.

The Trimesters of Pregnancy

Pregnancy has three trimesters, or parts. Each trimester has certain events and common characteristics.

Trimester One: Weeks 1–12

Mood swings

Fatigue

Morning sickness, or upset stomach

Swollen and tender breasts

Increased vaginal discharge and need to urinate

Fetal heartbeat heard at 10 to 20 weeks

Trimester Two: Weeks 13–27

Abdomen area is enlarging

Fetal movements felt after 16–20 weeks

Fatigue or nausea may have faded

Possible increased heartburn or indigestion

Possible constipation

Occasional headaches, faintness, or dizziness

Trimester Three: Weeks 28–Delivery

Physical discomfort, including backache, increases

Baby's size and weight may affect mother's balance and posture

Pressure on the mother's bladder makes urination more frequent

The baby's kicking may become more uncomfortable

Sexual activity and sleep become more difficult

Fatigue and frustration may increase

A recommended schedule for prenatal visits during pregnancy

8 weeks pregnant	First appointment
8–35 weeks pregnant	Every 4 weeks
36–38 weeks pregnant	Every 2 weeks
39 or more weeks pregnant	Weekly until birth

A doctor needs to determine a pregnant woman's health. The doctor will ask if the mother smokes, drinks alcohol, or uses other drugs. It is important to answer these questions honestly. The mother may have a test for HIV, the virus that causes AIDS. The doctor also may check for other sexually transmitted diseases. A doctor needs to know about the mother's eating habits. All of this information helps a doctor determine possible risks to the fetus.

Harmful Effects on the Fetus

Many things can harm a fetus. The father's situation or behaviors can harm the fetus. For example, the father's exposure to dangerous chemicals at work can harm his sperm. A male's use of drugs also can harm his sperm. In such cases, genetic problems may occur when the sperm and egg meet. That means the baby can be born with problems or unusual characteristics. Infections in the father can be passed to the mother. Sexually transmitted diseases during pregnancy may cause the baby to be born too early.

A young mother's behavior also can hurt the fetus. Drinking alcohol during pregnancy can cause fetal alcohol syndrome. This means that the baby may be born with unusual facial features. The child also may have trouble learning in school and throughout life. Alcohol is very dangerous to a fetus.

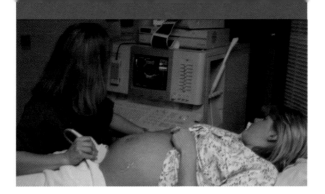

If a mother smokes, a baby can weigh too little at birth. Babies who are born small are more likely to have infections. Their lungs may not develop properly. These problems also can happen if the pregnant mother breathes in second-hand smoke from other smokers.

Kailee, Age 19

My pregnancy has been really rough. I threw up every day for the first three months. I couldn't eat much. My doctor was not worried. He was more worried about me not drinking. I got pregnant during a drinking binge. I don't remember having sex at all. I blacked out. It seems like I had been drunk for the last two years of my life. I started drinking in the morning when I was 16. I experimented with marijuana and speed, but I preferred drinking.

I started AA a week after I found out I was pregnant. I have a six-month medal for sobriety. I needed to get new friends— ones that didn't party. I quit my regular school. I was accepted into Sobriety High. It helps kids stay clean.

My doctor is really proud of me. He sends me postcards to cheer me on. I may choose adoption for my baby. It is such a hard decision. At least I know I'm giving my baby a good start.

Fast Fact

Learning healthy ways to relax and relieve stress increases the chances of having a healthy baby.

Dealing With Addictions

Some teens have addictions. These may include dependence on tobacco, alcohol, or other drugs. Addictions to alcohol and other drugs often lead to an unplanned pregnancy. Alcohol and other drugs affect a person's thinking and behavior. This impaired thinking can hinder use of pregnancy prevention methods.

A pregnant teen with an addiction needs to seek help. She is no longer dealing with the addiction alone. A baby is growing inside her. The addiction affects not only the mother but also the fetus.

Many young women seek help for addictions during pregnancy. They can learn how to stop using tobacco, alcohol, or other drugs.

A mother's drug addictions can cause a baby great harm. A baby often is born addicted to the drug that the mother uses. A baby's small body craves the drug, too. The baby's heart rate is affected. Drugs also can affect brain development in a baby. A baby whose mother has a drug addiction can be born early or be small at birth.

A school counselor, doctor, or therapist can help teens find effective programs for addiction problems. These programs have support groups and sessions to help teens overcome their addiction.

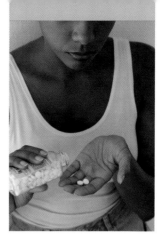

Other Common Dangers

Other things can harm a fetus. Pregnant women should avoid having unnecessary x-rays. Exposure to x-rays can cause birth defects. A pregnant woman should be careful about use of all medicines. She should take them only under a doctor's approval or direction. It is also important to read the labels on all medicines.

Lead has been shown to cause learning problems in children. Lead may be in the paint in older homes. It also may be in water that flows through old pipes. A local utility company can help test for lead.

Points to Consider

Describe how the use of drugs or alcohol could increase the risk of pregnancy.

How does a father's behavior affect the normal development of a fetus?

How does fetal alcohol syndrome occur in a baby?

Name two common dangers that can harm a fetus.

Chapter Overview

Pregnant teens can take childbirth classes to prepare for birth. A coach or partner is recommended for these classes.

Birth includes three stages: labor, pushing and delivery of the baby, and delivery of the placenta, or afterbirth.

Babies are born either by vaginal birth or cesarean section.

Chapter 4

The Birth

Mothers prepare for birth in a variety of ways. Most soon-to-be mothers sign up for a childbirth class. Childbirth classes help teens to understand what is going to happen. The classes teach about stages of labor, breathing exercises, and types of delivery. In one class, mothers may see an actual birth on videotape. In another class, they may visit the hospital's birthing rooms.

A miscarriage is the end of pregnancy before the twentieth week. A woman should call her doctor immediately if she experiences any of the following:

- Pain or cramps in the center of the lower abdomen and bleeding
- Severe, constant pain that lasts for more than one day, even without bleeding
- Bleeding as heavy as a menstrual period or a light staining occurs for more than three days
- Passing gray or pink clots

Instructors of childbirth classes suggest that mothers have a partner or coach. The partner is sometimes the baby's father. A childbirth class is a good way for a father to get involved. He can learn about the pregnancy and birth. Teen mothers, however, can use many people as a coach. They may ask a parent or a trusted friend or relative.

Women visit the doctor weekly in their last month of pregnancy. The doctor does a pelvic, or internal, exam. This exam checks the cervix, which is the opening to the uterus. The cervix must open for a baby to be born.

A doctor may request an ultrasound. This picture shows the position of the fetus in the uterus. Taking the picture is not harmful. It also can show the gender of the baby. Many parents like to know beforehand if the baby is a boy or a girl. Others like to be surprised at the time of the birth. An ultrasound picture is on the next page.

Stages of Labor

Labor, or childbirth, is the way in which a baby leaves its mother's uterus and is born. It is not clear how childbirth is triggered.

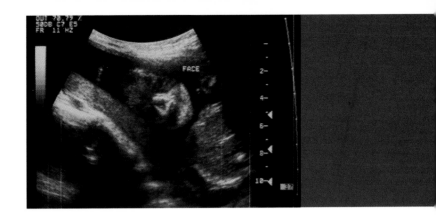

The length of labor can vary with each woman. The average time is 12 to 15 hours for a first baby. However, it can be much shorter or longer than this. There are three stages of labor.

Stage One: Early or Latent Labor Phase I

Stage One is usually the longest stage. It can last days or weeks. The mother's cervix becomes slightly dilated, or opened, to about 3 centimeters. Her body is preparing to release the baby.

Many pregnant women have contractions during this stage. This tightening of the uterus can be painful. The pain usually does not last more than 30 to 45 seconds. The contractions may occur at any time and are not constant.

Stage One: Active Labor Phase II

Phase II is shorter than phase I. A woman goes to the hospital during active labor. One sign of active labor is that the water sac surrounding the baby breaks. The sac may or may not break in this stage. Once the sac breaks, babies must be delivered within 24 hours in order to avoid infection.

Another sign of active labor is heavy contractions. The contractions may last 40 to 60 seconds. They may be three to four minutes apart. This stage can last from a few minutes up to four hours. It varies with every woman.

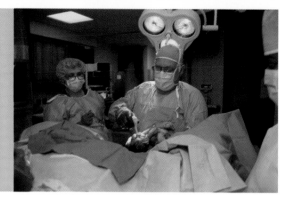

Stage One: Advanced Active Labor Phase III

Advanced labor is the most difficult but shortest stage. It typically lasts between 15 and 60 minutes. Contractions can last 60 to 90 seconds and stay peaked longer. A machine monitors the contractions. The pain is intense. Many women use the breathing exercises they learned in childbirth classes. The mother's birthing partner can help her through the pain.

Stage Two: Pushing and Delivery

Babies are born two different ways. A vaginal birth is most common. The woman pushes the baby out of her uterus. The baby moves through the cervix into the vagina. Each contraction helps the baby move along. Many women feel like the baby is coming out of their bottom. It feels like a painful bowel movement. Women also may experience back pain during labor.

Sometimes a woman needs an episiotomy. The doctor or midwife makes a cut in the skin next to the vagina. The cut prevents the area from tearing open. The episiotomy allows the baby more room to pass through the vagina. Not all women have an episiotomy.

Many women choose to receive pain medication. This helps ease the pain of birth.

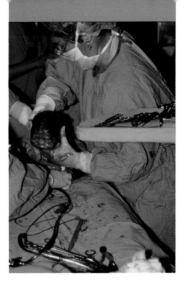

The baby is born during this stage. The woman may feel a strong urge to push. Some mothers may feel a renewed energy. The doctor or midwife tells her when it is time to push. This pushing births the baby. It may last a few minutes to a few hours. It varies with each mother.

Stage Three: Delivery of the Placenta
Women actually birth two things during labor and delivery. First, the baby is born. Second, the placenta, or afterbirth, is pushed through the birth canal. The placenta provides food to the baby during pregnancy.

A vaginal birth has a short recovery period. The nurses at the hospital massage the abdomen to help it shrink. Many women may take baths to help heal the episiotomy. New mothers and their baby usually go home within 48 hours after the birth.

A Cesarean Birth
The second way a baby is born is cesarean section. This delivery is done in an operating room. The doctor cuts through the abdomen and uterus. The mother receives a strong pain medicine. She cannot feel anything on the lower half of her body. She can be awake during the surgery.

A doctor chooses cesarean delivery to avoid problems or harm for mother or baby or both. A cesarean birth is not easier and less painful for the mother than vaginal birth. It is only done for medical reasons that make a vaginal delivery unsafe. For example, the birth canal may be too small. Another reason is that the baby may go into distress during birth. A third reason is that the baby may be in a breech position. A breech position means the baby's buttocks and legs come out first. Babies are usually born headfirst.

A cesarean birth has a longer recovery period than a vaginal birth does. It is major surgery. Mothers cannot lift heavy objects for several weeks. They are not supposed to lift the baby. They need a lot of help around home. It is important that the mother try not to do too much during her recovery.

After the Birth

After birth, the baby's umbilical cord must be cut. This cord serves as a lifeline between the mother and fetus during pregnancy. After birth, it is tied off with a small plastic pin. This area becomes the belly button, or navel.

Suggestions for care of the umbilical cord stump:

- Keep the area dry.
- Avoid tub baths until the cord has fallen off.
- Expose the area.
- Keep the diaper turned down and the shirt area open when possible.
- Clean the cord stump with alcohol.
- Use lotion to keep the surrounding skin moist.

During a normal delivery, the baby is usually placed on the mother's chest. The baby starts the shift from life inside to life outside the uterus. The mother begins to care for her baby in a different way.

Points to Consider

Why is it a good idea for a pregnant woman to take a childbirth class?

Describe how labor begins.

How would a woman's coach or partner help during labor and delivery?

How do you think teens can learn to connect the act of sex with future parenting?

Chapter Overview

Some new mothers feel sad or depressed. This postpartum depression is a normal stage after childbirth. It is important for mothers to know when to ask for help when they have postpartum depression.

New mothers must decide between breast-feeding or bottle-feeding. Most doctors agree breast-feeding has more benefits than bottle-feeding.

New mothers need to learn about the care of a newborn. This includes learning to diaper, feed, and help the baby develop good sleeping patterns.

Parent-child attachment is an indicator for a child's future. Healthy attachment depends on consistent care.

Baby books provide new parents with information about normal child development.

Chapter 5

After the Birth and Caring for a Newborn

Postpartum Depression

Women often have feelings of depression or deep sadness after childbirth. This postpartum depression usually lasts a few days. It results from changing hormone levels. Women with postpartum depression may feel exhausted. The struggles of labor and delivery catch up with the mother. Yet she must continue with daily life. She also must care for her new baby. It is important for new mothers to know when to ask for help.

Some women become depressed because they have gained weight. This weight gain is normal. It takes months for the body to recover. A light exercise routine can begin after birth. The routine can build gradually to more active exercise.

Some mothers can become overly concerned with their appearance. They may complain about their body. New mothers, however, need to focus on the baby. A baby needs the mother's full attention. A woman's body recovers over time.

Janelle, Age 18

I didn't gain much weight when I was pregnant. I had a hard time quitting smoking, too. Cecilia was born six weeks early. She was in the hospital for a month until she could breath on her own.

My doctor and social worker taught me a lot. They started me in parenting classes. I learned how to hold and feed Cecilia when she barely weighed four pounds. I've been forced to make different choices. I have to focus on Cecilia. She needs me to be a good mom.

Support for the New Mother

Many women feel unprepared to be a mother. The mother often has to get up in the night. Her sleep may be disturbed for feedings or because her baby cries or vomits. This is why it is important to have a good support system. It helps to include an experienced mother in a support system. She can be the expert for questions about newborn babies. She can share useful information about child care and self-care.

Newborn Babies

A newborn baby is fragile. The baby can't roll over or hold its head up. A baby's neck needs to be supported when he or she is picked up and held. Being wrapped securely in blankets gives a baby a safe and secure feeling.

A person's belly button is formed in the first few weeks of life. The remains of the umbilical cord are still attached to the baby's abdomen. The cord stump must be cleaned with rubbing alcohol each time a diaper is changed. This helps the cord to dry up. It will fall off in one to two weeks.

Myth: Picking up a crying baby all the time will spoil him or her.

Fact: You cannot spoil an infant by responding to his or her cry. The baby learns trust when its caretaker consistently responds to its cry.

Breast-Feeding or Bottle-Feeding

A mother must decide between breast-feeding or bottle-feeding her baby. Often, a woman's decision is based on her own mother's choice. Doctors and researchers agree breast-feeding is the best choice for babies. Bottle-feeding, however, also has certain benefits. Here are some reasons for using either method.

Reasons to Breast-Feed	Reasons to Bottle-Feed
Milk made especially for baby	Baby feels full longer
Easy to digest	Easy to check how much milk the baby drinks
Less risk of allergy	More participation for the father
Helps baby to resist illness	Less stressful feeding in public
Convenient (no preparation)	
Costs nothing	
Easiest method, especially in the middle of the night	

Feeding time is a special time between mother and baby. The close contact helps the mother bond with her baby in the first days of life. Bonding is largely the parent's experience. Over time, however, the baby will attach to the mother.

Mother-Child Attachment

Attachment is important to the long-term development of a baby. Babies communicate through their cries. Each cry has a different message. Parents who respond consistently help build a good attachment with their baby. This good attachment is the foundation for a child's self-esteem.

Diapers and Bowel Movements

A newborn soils many diapers. New babies may use a dozen diapers a day. A newborn fills diapers with a tarry black substance during the first few days. This substance is from a build-up in the intestines during the stay in the uterus.

Breast-fed babies have loose, mustard-colored stools. Bottle-fed babies have more formed stools. The color is pale yellow to brownish.

Diapers need to be changed regularly. This prevents diaper rash. It also helps to keep the baby comfortable. Diaper rash can be treated with ointments. Many mothers use baby powder to keep the baby's bottom dry. Powder, however, can affect the baby's breathing system. It is best not to use baby powder.

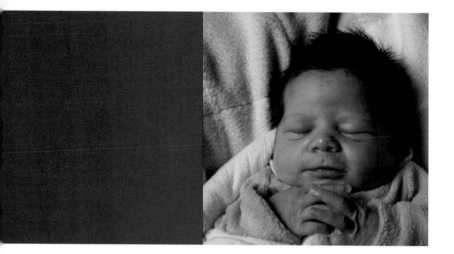

Sleeping

Newborns sleep much of the time. Eventually, they develop regular sleep patterns. Parents can help develop healthy routines for sleep.

Babies should be put to bed on their side or their back, not lying on their belly face down. This is a safer way for babies to sleep. It reduces the risk of sudden infant death syndrome (SIDS), or crib death. It is also good to put babies in bed when they are still a little bit awake. They learn how to fall asleep this way.

A baby can be prepared for bedtime with gentle talk and a quiet room. Babies enjoy close contact and warmth. Bedtime is a good time for the father to build an attachment with his baby.

Babies who live in loud, chaotic homes may have a hard time learning to sleep. Sleep patterns may not develop. When possible, a baby should have regular nap and sleeping times. This provides structure around a baby's schedule.

2 weeks	Newborn checkup
2, 4, 6, and 15 months	Physical exam and immunizations
10 months	Physical exam, blood work, and immunizations
2 years	Physical exam
3½ years	Physical exam and vision screening

Child Development

Baby and parenting books provide answers for many questions. The books describe normal child development. They give tips for toilet training. They describe common childhood diseases such as chickenpox. New mothers benefit from a good book on child care and development.

It is important to respect normal child development. For example, babies should not be fed solid foods too early. Babies sleep through the night when their body is ready. Also, a mother should resist comparing her baby with other babies. Each baby develops at its own rate and has its own special qualities.

Points to Consider

Why do women have feelings of depression after childbirth?

How can an experienced mother help support a new mother?

How could a parent make diapering and feeding a time of love for a baby?

How would you deal with the birth of a baby born with special needs or birth defects?

Chapter Overview

Raising a child is expensive. Teen moms must learn different ways to manage and budget their money.

A young mother must plan for her future. She should make decisions about school, job training, or full-time work in the best interest of her new family.

Most mothers need help with child care. There are important things to look for in a good day care provider.

Babies should not be physically punished. Spanking is an adult's violent response.

A parent who reads, talks, and plays with a baby helps prepare the child for school.

Chapter 6

Raising a Baby

Babies are expensive. Diapers, formula, and clothes are daily needs. A new baby also needs a crib, car seat, stroller, and other equipment. A hospital birth alone costs about $2,000. Most teens are covered under one or both parents' health insurance. Some teens need to use public assistance funds. Young mothers need to be creative in finding ways to pay expenses.

A Budget

Learning to keep a budget can be an important task for a new mother. Many teen mothers learn tricks to save money. They learn how to use coupons. They know about good sales. They may shop at garage sales. Another option is second-hand stores. Used clothing is more affordable than new clothing. Babies grow out of clothes quickly. Used baby clothing usually looks close to new.

Balancing School or Work

Mothers need an income in order to use a budget. Government money, such as welfare, may only support mothers for two to five years. Young mothers must plan for their future. The first step is finishing high school. Many youth receive job training in high school. Others complete specialized training after high school.

Young women have many choices for job training. Some attend vocational training where they learn a specific skill. Others attend a two-year college to earn an associate degree. Still others attend a four-year college. Each additional year of school increases a person's income possibilities.

Full-time work is also an option. Teen mothers may begin working at a job that requires no special training. This may bring in a quick income. Some employers provide money for schooling. Other employers train their workers for management jobs. Many options may be available within a business or company.

Child Care

A young mother needs to help build her future. This takes time. Specifically, it is time away from her baby. One of the most important decisions a mother has is choosing good day care for her baby.

Things to look for in a day care provider:

- Licensing—How many years has the provider been licensed?
- Training—Does the provider have training in child development or rescue breathing?
- Environment—Does the area appear healthy and safe? Does the staff keep the carpet clean? Are hands washed regularly?
- Number of children—Does the provider appear to be able to meet the needs of her children? Are children crying? Do children have to wait for care?
- A loving feeling—Does the provider seem to like children? Do children seek out the provider for hugs and special attention?
- Open door—Are parents always welcome?

The day care provider is an important caretaker in the life of a child. The provider must give good care and ensure the child's safety. Parents, relatives, neighbors, or friends may help out with day care. Over time, however, this arrangement may be difficult to continue.

Finding a safe, affordable day care provider can be challenging. Many counties publish lists of licensed day care providers. Phone interviews are a way to begin the process of finding good day care. Home or day care site visits are important. The visits are useful to see how the provider works with children.

Day care is a reality for teen moms. It allows them to build a good future for their family. It allows young mothers to finish school and learn job skills. Day care usually is necessary so the mother, and possibly the father, can work to support the family. Day care can be a very positive experience for infants.

Stress and Discipline

Daily schedules with a baby can be hectic. Preparation is critical. Babies need diapers, bottles, a change of clothes, medicine, toys, and car seats. The mom must organize her own life as well.

Stress can be high for mother and baby. It is important to remember that crying is the only form of communication for a baby. Cries may mean hunger, wet diapers, sickness, tiredness, or a need to be held. Parents who promptly respond to their babies teach security.

Good parents understand discipline. They learn how to be patient with children. They know never to spank a baby. Spanking is an angry response to a child. It teaches children to be violent. Babies should never be spanked.

A mother who is frustrated and strikes a child puts the child at risk. Mothers who parent alone must recognize their stress limits. A parent, friend, neighbor, or the baby's father can help. Most mothers need to take short breaks from parenting. Mothers who love their children avoid putting the baby at risk.

Preparing for School—Already?

A mother's relationship with a baby begins at conception. Success can begin with the care a mother takes during pregnancy. As the child grows, the mother continues to build care and support for the baby.

Reading is a lifelong skill. Parents who read newspapers, books, or magazines model the importance of reading. Reading helps to build success in school for a child.

Did You Know?

One of the things I remember about growing up was books. My parents always read to me. I had my own bag to carry my books. I read to my son when he was still in my belly. I told him stories and talked to him all the time. When he was born last year, the first thing I bought him was a Dr. Seuss book.

Abbey, Age 17

He is six months old now. He babbles at the books that I read him. He stares at the pictures. He loves to hear me read. It is really a special time for us.

Reading and speaking are important foundations for school. Parents who talk to their babies help build future language skills. Children who are read to as babies and toddlers have higher reading abilities. Success in school tends to be easier for these children.

Points to Consider

What could a teen mother do to save money after the birth of a baby?

What advice would you give a teen mother about planning for her future? Would you encourage college, full-time work, or another option? Why?

Create a list of questions to ask a potential child care provider.

Chapter Overview

Parents who put their child first work together. Many parents who do not live in the same home still work together to raise their child.

Most teen mothers do not get married.

Establishing paternity has benefits, including the right to ask for financial support.

A mother must put her child first and recognize risks and dangers to the child.

Chapter 7

Mother and Father Parenting Together

Children have many benefits when mom and dad work together as parents. Researchers believe that children are better off when many adults raise them. A parent faces many difficulties when raising a child alone. No other adult is around for daily support. There is only one income. Single parenting puts a lot of pressure on one person. It is not impossible. It is simply more difficult.

A teen mother may find it difficult to work with the father of her baby. Even so, she must think about her child first. Children can have a special relationship with their father. A good father teaches his children many important things. Mothers who foster this relationship help their children.

Parents can share the responsibility of raising their baby. They can share the expenses. It is important for both parents to be honest with each other about their feelings. Their romantic relationship may be over. Their parenting relationship, however, lasts for at least 18 years.

> When Darrance was born, me and Tony **Tamera, Age 19** weren't dating anymore. We hadn't talked for about four months. Tony showed up at the hospital after Darrance was born. He wanted to sign the Declaration of Parentage papers. I was glad he wanted to be part of Darrance's life. Every boy needs a dad around.
>
> Tony takes care of Darrance every weekend. I've been working as much as I can. Tony's mother has helped him, too. She has taught him how to change diapers and feed the baby. Tony pays child support. I get about $200 every month. It helps pay for day care mostly. I'm glad Tony is a big part of our son's life.

Establishing Paternity

Most teen mothers do not get married. In fact, 76 percent of teen mothers have their child outside of marriage. This makes the role of the father more difficult. He is only the legal father if paternity is established. The father of the child is determined when both parents sign legal forms. Many states allow teen parents to sign the Recognition of Parentage (or Declaration of Parentage) form at the hospital.

Half of all children born today will spend part of their childhood in a single-parent home.

Did You **Know?**

There are benefits to establishing paternity. One benefit is that the mother knows she is not solely responsible for raising the baby. Another benefit is that the mother can ask for child support. This money comes from the father to support the child. Most states automatically take money from a person's paycheck.

The Primary Home

Teen parents make many hard decisions. For example, parenting is often done in two different homes. The parents must decide together whose home will be the primary one for the baby. Young couples can still parent together even if they live apart. Children are better adjusted if the parents work together.

Sometimes a teen mother lives in the home of her parents. She also might live in the home of her boyfriend's parents. In either case, she raises the baby with an extra set of parents in one home. Teen parents need to set clear boundaries. The help of a teen's parent is great, but the teen is the baby's primary parent.

Custody

Parents who don't live in the same home still may share custody of the child. Perhaps only one parent has legal custody. He or she has the primary responsibility for decisions about the child. It helps if the couple views parenting as being business partners. Then they work together as a team in the business of caring for their child. They can use their strengths and skills to raise a healthy child together.

Car Seat Tips

- Infants must ride in their car seat, facing backward, until they weigh 20 pounds.
- The middle of the back seat is the safest place in the car.
- Children or infants should never be placed in the front seat of a car. This is especially true if the car has passenger-side air bags.
- Follow the manufacturer's instructions when installing a car seat.
- Check the seat buckles regularly to ensure they work.

Putting the Child First

Good mothers put the child first. This does not mean they let the child do whatever he or she wants. It means they put the needs of the child above their own needs. It means that mothers make sacrifices. A young mother may be angry with the father. She must learn to separate her anger with him from his role as a father.

Parents who value children work together to put the child first. They realize it benefits a child to grow up with two important relationships. The child learns how to get along with others. This happens when parents work as a team to raise healthy, well-adjusted children.

Providing a Safe Home

Parents also can work together to set up a safe house for children. Toddlers are naturally curious and explore a lot. Young children need to be taught about danger. Electrical outlets, candles, and chemicals are found in most homes. These things can be dangerous to young children. Parents need to provide a safe home by protecting children from these dangers.

Sometimes a parent can harm or hurt a child. For example, a parent who is violent is a danger to a child. A parent who has a drug or alcohol addiction also can be a risk. A parent involved in criminal activity can be dangerous. The primary parent must recognize these risks.

Parents who are a danger to a child may need to stay away. For example, teen mothers may have to keep a father from his child legally. It is important for the mother to write down examples of the danger. Witnesses to the danger also should record what they have seen. The police or a social worker can use this information. They can keep the father away until he is healthy.

Points to Consider

Name several challenges teens may face when parenting together.

How does establishing paternity benefit the mother?

What kinds of sacrifices must teen parents make when parenting?

How do parents put a baby at risk?

Chapter Overview

It helps a teen mom to make a plan for the future. The plan should include a strong support system.

Teen mothers who finish their education can provide a better future for their child. Education increases job choices.

Pregnancy prevention methods are part of future plans. Abstinence is an effective choice.

Fathers are important to children. Teen mothers should try to nurture their child's relationship with the father.

Teen mothers can make a commitment to raising a happy, healthy baby.

Chapter 8

Your Future— Making It Work for You

Teen mothers have a lot of responsibility. They must make daily and future plans and set goals. They learn a lot along the way. Nothing is more important than raising their child.

Make a Plan

Future plans involve many choices. A teen mother's immediate plans should center on the baby. Daily care and child development are most important. Understanding child development and learning to love and nurture the baby are the key. Plans should include regular doctor visits. These visits help monitor the health and growth of a child. Immunizations are part of doctor visits. These shots protect a child from disease or sickness.

Education and Career Choices

Completing high school is a crucial first step in future plans. A second step in future plans is setting career goals. A career choice is not a lifelong commitment. It is the beginning of several job choices.

A Strong Support System

All new mothers need support. A teen mother especially needs a strong support system. A mentor can help a teen mom be a better parent. Mentors are people with experience. They make good listeners. They know when a young mother needs support and a hug. Mentors can give a young mother a break when she needs it. They can help a teen mom make decisions about her future.

Effective Pregnancy Prevention

Teen mothers must make decisions about their sexual activity. They also must decide about consistent use of a birth control method to prevent pregnancy. Most methods work well if used consistently and correctly. Instructions are included with most methods. Young women can learn about these methods from a health care provider.

Pregnancy Prevention Options

Nonprescription

1   Male condom—A thin latex or polyurethane covering that fits over the penis to catch sperm. Most effective when used with a spermicide. Also protects against sexually transmitted diseases.

2   Female condom—A bag-like piece of polyurethane that fits inside the vagina. Helps to prevent pregnancy by keeping sperm out of the uterus. Also protects against sexually transmitted diseases.

3   Spermicide—A foam, cream, tablet, or gel put into the vagina to kill sperm. When used correctly together, condoms and spermicides are 97 percent effective in preventing pregnancy.

Prescription

1   Birth control pills—A daily pill that prevents an egg from being released each month.

2   Progestin—A drug given to a woman to prevent an egg from being released each month. Progestin can be given in the form of pills, as a shot, or implanted under the skin.

3   Emergency contraceptive pill (morning after pill)—A combination of tablets that provides emergency birth control when used immediately after unprotected sex or within 72 hours. This is not meant to be an ongoing birth control method. It will not work if implantation of the fertilized egg has occurred.

4   Diaphragm—A rubber cup placed over the cervix to keep sperm out of the uterus. Must be used with a spermicide and a male condom.

Couples who are sexually active should talk about parenting and pregnancy prevention. One in four teen moms has a second child again within two years. A second child doubles the expenses. Using pregnancy prevention allows a mother to plan future pregnancies.

William was born when I was seventeen. I had been dating his father for a year. We had been careful most of the time. Sometimes we just didn't care. That's when I got pregnant. William's father dropped me so fast. I was angry. I thought he would marry me.

Tysley, Age 19

When William was born, his father called. I told him about William. His father wanted to know if we could talk. Then he wanted to know if we could start dating again. I said no, but I knew it was important for William to know his father.

He is a good dad to William. We get along really well as parents. We talk and laugh about William all the time. I haven't dated since William was born. I know I will again, but now is not the right time. Sex is just not part of my plan right now. I can't afford another pregnancy. It wouldn't be fair to William.

The likelihood of having intercourse increases steadily with age. One in five teens, however, does not have intercourse during the teenage years.

Fast **Fact**

Abstinence

Some women choose abstinence. They make a choice not to have sexual intercourse. This is an effective method of preventing a pregnancy. Choosing abstinence avoids both an unplanned pregnancy and sexually transmitted diseases.

The Father's Involvement

Teen mothers can help build the father's involvement with their child. They should not use the child as a threat. They should never put the child in the middle of an argument with the father. Good mothers learn to communicate with the father. They learn to make compromises. Finally, they recognize the important role a father plays in the life of a child.

Making the Commitment

Teen pregnancy can become a cycle. Many teen mothers were born to women who also were mothers in their teens. Many risk factors make it hard for teen mothers to parent well. Therefore, young women must work hard to break the cycle of teen pregnancy. Young women can:

• Be a good role model for their child.
• Choose a healthy lifestyle.
• Take child development and parenting classes.
• Learn how to keep a budget.
• Read and talk to their baby.
• Love their baby.

Raising a baby is a challenge. Babies are like clay. They need their parents to help them take form. A teen mother can help in shaping her baby's life. Time spent with the baby helps give the child a healthy attachment.

Raising a child takes patience and sacrifice. It takes hard work. Yet there is nothing more rewarding to a parent than a happy, healthy child.

Points to Consider

Why might it be hard for a teen mother to make a plan for her future?

How easy do you think it would be for a teen mom to abstain from sex after having a baby?

Describe ways a teen mother can support the father's relationship with his baby.

What qualities do you think are important in good parents? How does a teen mother learn these qualities?

Glossary

addiction (uh-DIK-shuhn)—dependence on something, such as a drug

cervix (sur-VIKS)—the narrow outer opening of the uterus

child support (CHILDE suh-PORT)—money paid by a parent to support a child

conception (kuhn-SEP-shuhn)—union of a male sperm with a female egg to form a human being

contraceptive (kon-truh-SEP-tiv)—something that prevents conception

contraction (kuhn-TRAK-shuhn)—a tightening of the uterus

dilation (dye-LAY-shuhn)—the slow opening of the cervix

episiotomy (uh-PEE-zee-OT-tuhm-ee)—a small cut intended to give a baby more room to pass through the vagina during childbirth

fetus (FEE-tuhss)—an unborn, developing human being

hormone (HOR-mohn)—a chemical that controls a body function

immunization (IM-yuh-nye-zay-shuhn)—making the body able to resist certain diseases

paternity (puh-TUR-nuh-tee)—being a father

physical custody (FIZ-uh-kuhl KUHSS-tuh-dee)—the parent who makes decisions for and has daily care of a child

prenatal care (pree-NAY-tuhl KAIR)—a pregnant woman's regular doctor visits before a baby is born

sexual intercourse (SEK-shoo-uhl IN-tur-korss)—penetration of the penis into the vagina

umbilical cord (uhm-BIL-uh-kuhl KORD)—tube that connects a fetus to the mother during pregnancy

For More Information

Arthur, Shirley M., and Jeanne W. Lindsay. *Surviving Teen Pregnancy: Your Choices, Dreams, Decisions.* Buena Park, CA: Morning Glory Press, 1996.

Barr, Linda, and Catherine Monserrat. *Teenage Pregnancy: A New Beginning.* Albuquerque, NM: New Futures, 1996.

Eisenberg, Arlene, Heidi Eisenberg Murkoff, and Sandee Eisenberg Hathaway. *What to Expect the First Year.* New York: Workman, 1996.

Eisenberg, Arlene, Heidi Eisenberg Murkoff, and Sandee Eisenberg Hathaway. *What to Expect When You're Expecting.* New York: Workman, 1996.

Endersbe, Julie K. *Teen Pregnancy: Tough Choices.* Mankato, MN: Capstone Press, 2000.

Useful Addresses and Internet Sites

Alan Guttmacher Institute
120 Wall Street
New York, NY 10005
www.agi-usa.org

Campaign to Prevent Teen Pregnancy
2100 M Street Northwest, Suite 300
Washington, DC 20037
www.teenpregnancy.org

Canadian Public Health Association
National AIDS Clearinghouse
1565 Carling Ave., Suite 400
Ottawa, ON K1Z 8R1
CANADA

Planned Parenthood Federation of America
810 Seventh Avenue
New York, NY 10019
1-800-230-7526
www.plannedparenthood.org

Planned Parenthood Federation of Canada
1 Nicholas Street, Suite 430
Ottawa, ON K1N 7B7
CANADA
www.ppfc.ca

The Baby Place
www.baby-place.com
Information for parents on pregnancy, birth, and babies

Federal Office of Child Support Enforcement
www.acf.dhhs.gov/programs/cse/index.html
Provides information on state child support enforcement guidelines

National Child Care Information Center
www.nccic.org
A resource for parents who need more information about finding child care

Parenthood Web
www.parenthoodweb.com
Pediatricians and psychiatrists respond to questions from parents

teenwire
www.teenwire.com
Sexuality and relationship information for teens

Index

Index continued